Pub Walks

Laurie Page

COUNTRYSIDE BOOKS
NEWBURY BERKSHIRE

First published 2022

© 2022 Laurie Page

COUNTRYSIDE BOOKS
3 Catherine Road
Newbury, Berkshire

To view our complete range of books,
please visit us at
www.countrysidebooks.co.uk

ISBN 978 1 84674 409 9

*All materials used in the production of this book
carry FSC certification.*

Produced through The Letterworks Ltd., Reading
Typeset by KT Designs, St Helens
Printed by Holywell Press, Oxford

Introduction

I was delighted to have the opportunity to write this *Guide to Somerset Pub Walks*, so that I could explore more of this diverse and interesting county. There is the pretty coast, the Somerset Levels, Exmoor National Park, the Quantock and Mendip Hills, not to mention numerous villages and towns of character. Some walks appear to be short in distance, but due to the hilly Somerset terrain there are some challenging and steep climbs here, and the views from the top make it worthwhile.

At the end of each walk there's a welcoming pub where you can sit in comfort with a drink and some tasty food if you wish to stay for a meal. Also included with each walk are suggestions for nearby attractions, such as historic buildings, museums, wildlife parks and steam railways. As you've no doubt noticed, the book is perfectly sized so that it will fit easily into your pocket. So, whatever the season, get out there and enjoy these Somerset rambles.

Laurie Page

Publisher's Note

We hope that you obtain considerable enjoyment from this book; great care has been taken in its preparation. Although at the time of publication all routes followed public rights of way or permitted paths, diversion orders can be made and permissions withdrawn.

We cannot, of course, be held responsible for such diversion orders or any inaccuracies in the text which result from these or any other changes to the routes, nor any damage which might result from walkers trespassing on private property. We are anxious, though, that all the details covering the walks are kept up to date, and would therefore welcome information from readers which would be relevant to future editions.

The simple sketch maps that accompany the walks in this book are based on notes made by the author whilst surveying the routes on the ground. They are designed to show you how to reach the start and to point out the main features of the overall circuit, and they contain a progression of numbers that relate to the paragraphs of the text.

However, for the benefit of a proper map, we do recommend that you purchase the relevant Ordnance Survey sheet covering your walk. Ordnance Survey maps are widely available, especially through booksellers and local newsagents.

1 Winsford

5¾ miles (9.2 km)

WALK HIGHLIGHTS

This walk takes you to the heart of Exmoor. The route follows the River Exe to the hamlet of Exton, nestled amongst the rolling hills, woodland, brooks and streams of this beautiful National Park.

THE PUB

The Royal Oak Exmoor, Halse Lane, TA24 7JE.
☎ 01643 851455 www.royaloakexmoor.co.uk
Traditional village inn complete with thatched roof, restaurant, bar, hotel and even a Post Office.

THE WALK

1 From the parking area go right along the road past the red telephone box and take the next left, **West Howetown Lane**, a no through road going over the **River Exe**. Go up to the end of the lane and through the

Guide to Somerset Pub Walks

START: Edbrooke Road, Winsford. **Sat Nav:** TA24 7JE.

PARKING: Small parking area by the road junction in the centre of the village.

MAP: OS Explorer OL9 Exmoor. **Grid Ref:** SS906349.

TERRAIN: Mostly good paths but many ups and downs. The byway at the end of the walk is often wet and muddy so robust, waterproof footwear is necessary.

wooden gate on the right. Turn right onto the bridleway to **Coppleham**. Go down the sunken path, through gates, down through the trees to the river. Continue along by the riverbank, which swings left, through more gates. At the 'private property' sign on the metal gate, go left up a steep bank, through a gate and along by a wire fence. The path goes straight on along the ridge, then right down to cross a track. Turn right at the next track down to the road.

2 Turn left along the road to the T-junction, and then right along the main road. After a short distance turn left onto a restricted byway going up between banks. Cross a pretty stream then another and proceed up to the houses. Follow a concrete track to the right, bringing you to a road by a telephone box. Turn left, then immediately left again along a public right of way which passes **Exton church**. Go down and cross left over the stream, then back uphill. Enjoy the views at the top. After another gate you reach **Widlake Farm**.

3 Go through the farm buildings and look out for a sign to the right, taking you up through a wooden farm gate and then a metal gate. At the next gate you leave the track, going left along the field to more gates where you turn right, downhill amongst the ferns, then at the next gate bear left going very steeply down to a metal gate. Cross the brook and turn right through a gate, then bear left to the cottage by a gate.

4 Turn left and keep left of the garden, through a gate and straight across a field. Then keep straight ahead into two more fields, passing through a gate into an area of scrub which leads to a stile and bridge by the

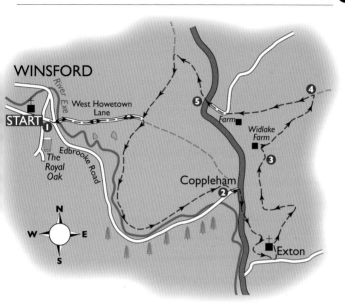

farm. Go left around the farm then left up the access road to the lane. Keep left, leading to the main road. Take the byway opposite.

❺ The path goes right, up what is usually a soggy track. Continue uphill for some distance, through a gate and up until you reach a path junction, where you turn left. Turn left again at the next junction, signed to **West Howetown**. Go through a gate and continue all the way down to eventually reach **West Howetown Lane**. Turn right and retrace your steps to return to the village parking area.

PLACES OF INTEREST NEARBY

Exmoor has abundant wildlife and to the south-west is the **Tarr Steps Woodland Nature Reserve**. Red deer, wild ponies, otters, squirrels, bird life and butterflies abound.

2 Minehead

4 miles (6.5 km)

WALK HIGHLIGHTS
This is a beautiful seaside walk along part of the South West Coast Path on the edge of the Exmoor National Park. There are spectacular views of the coast, town and countryside at various points along the way.

THE PUB
The Old Ship Aground, Quay Street, TA24 5UL.
☎ 01643 703516 www.theoldshipaground.com
Edwardian harbourside pub with wood fires and cosy atmosphere, serving locally sourced produce. Open seven days a week.

THE WALK
1 From the car parking area by **The Old Ship Aground**, head west away from the town to the end of the road where there is a mini roundabout. Go through the wooden gate to **Culvercliffe Walk**, past the children's play area. Follow the concrete path to a shady route through the trees, soon going steeply uphill, for some distance. Proceed along the coastal footpath which later goes gently down to join a vehicular access lane. Enter the National Trust land and just before the cottage turn

START: Quay Street, Minehead. **Sat Nav:** TA24 5UH.

PARKING: Pay & display car park and bays on Quay Street. For free parking head to North Hill Burgandy Combe car park where you can start and finish the walk at point 3, TA24 5LB.

MAP: OS Explorer OL9 Exmoor. **Grid Ref:** SS971468.

TERRAIN: No stiles. Good paths but very steep upward climbs during the first half of the walk.

off onto the footpath going uphill on the left, signed to **North Hill**, (**South West Coast Path**).

2 The path bends sharply right and then left and goes up very steeply along the side of the tree-covered hill. Go through a wooden gate and up to a path junction by a bench. Turn right, still going uphill but less steeply, on a good wide path which runs for over ½ mile. The route changes to a more open aspect with sea views to the left. Proceed to a little crossroads of footpaths where you turn left going steeply up to another bench by a signpost. Go straight ahead through the car park and out onto the road.

3 Turn left along the road. There are wonderful views both left and right. Pass another car park on the left and a bridleway on the right. Continue gently down to turn left onto a bridleway, signed to **Moor Wood**. At the path junction soon after, the bridleway bends right past a cattle grid. Proceed down the wide track through woodland. At the next path junction turn right (almost going back on yourself) signed to **Higher Town**.

4 The path descends and bends sharply left going steeply down. Keep to the main track going downward. This bends left then right taking you to the road. Turn left along the lane. Pass **Moor Road**, then thatched cottages and the beautiful **St Michael's church**. The road bends left. Join a pavement past **Marston Lodge hotel**. At the war memorial (which has a seat with views of the bay) go straight ahead at the junction down **Weirfield Road**.

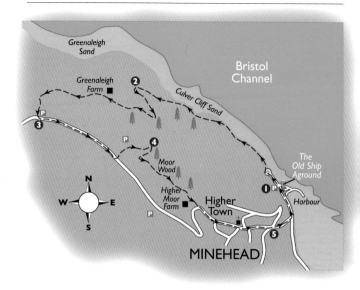

5 Follow the pavement to the end and at the path junction turn right. Take a left down steps through a gap in the fence. Turn left by the seat down more steps, then left again down the steps to the coast road. Go left along the road which returns you to the harbour and the parking area by the pub.

PLACES OF INTEREST NEARBY

Minehead is a traditional seaside resort with a sandy beach, and a lifeboat station by the harbour at the start of the walk. A few minutes from Quay Street is **Minehead Museum** at The Avenue. With free admission from March to October, it provides a potted history of the town with many local exhibits. Almost opposite the museum is the station for the **West Somerset Railway**, a 22-mile heritage railway with both diesel and steam engines.

Dunster Castle

3 Dunster
3 miles (5 km)

WALK HIGHLIGHTS
On this walk into history, you'll head into the hills above Dunster to the site of an Iron Age hillfort, over 2,000 years old. It's obvious why our ancestors chose this site; the scenery is spectacular, with views for miles around. Keep an eye out for Exmoor ponies, deer and other wildlife.

THE PUB
The Foresters Arms, West Street, TA24 6SN.
☎ 01643 821313 www.foresters-arms-dunster.co.uk
Family- and dog-friendly pub with a traditional British menu, right in the heart of Dunster.

THE WALK
1 Turn left out of the car park and cross the **River Avill** by the old stone bridge. Go straight on past the thatched cottage and at the footpath

11

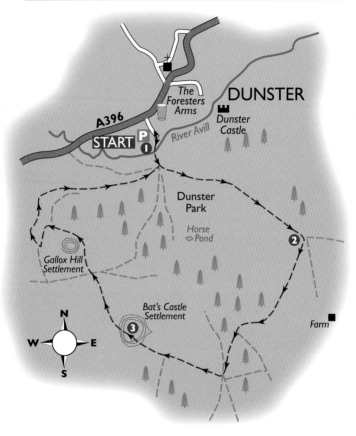

junction soon after, turn left (signed to **Carhampton**), through a gate. Keep left still following Carhampton, going gently uphill with good views of **Dunster Castle** to the left. Go through a gate by an old oak

START: Park Street, Dunster. **Sat Nav:** TA24 6SP.

PARKING: Pay & display car park at the end of Park Street.

MAP: OS Explorer OL9 Exmoor. **Grid Ref:** SS989432.

TERRAIN: A long upward gradient to reach the Iron Age hillfort halfway round. No stiles.

tree. Continue to the end of the field to another gate which leads to a footpath T-junction. Turn right onto a byway.

❷ Continue uphill along a wide stony thoroughfare. This is a long uphill climb. Pass a path on the left. When you reach the signpost by the bench, turn right through a gate (with an information board featuring Iron Age hillforts) and then go straight on, signed to **Bat's Castle**. At the next path junction go straight ahead; here the path narrows. When you cross a brook and go up a stony bank, you are inside the hillfort called Bat's Castle. Here you can enjoy the scenery and magnificent views all around.

❸ As you leave the fort you start to descend. Pass a path on the right and at the fork, bear left. You then go downhill steeply on a permissive path to go through a wooden gate (access on the right-hand side). The path swings left through the trees and ends at a path junction where you turn sharp right. At the viewpoint sign soon after, the path bends right going down eventually to a fork where you go right following the bridleway to **Dunster**. Continue for some distance going down all the way until you reach the path junction where you turn left and return to the car park via the stone bridge you crossed at the start of the walk.

PLACES OF INTEREST NEARBY

The splendid **Dunster Castle** on the edge of the village is owned by the National Trust. Built on a hill overlooking the village in early medieval times, there is a shop, café, bookshop and gardens. Next to the castle is a restored 18th-century watermill open to the public.

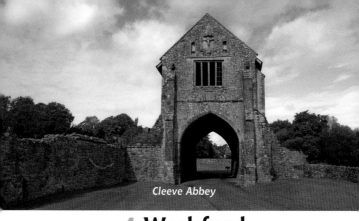

Cleeve Abbey

4 Washford

4 miles (6.4 km)

WALK HIGHLIGHTS

This route runs through rolling Somerset countryside then around Washford village and back via part of the Macmillan Way, with an excellent pub and an interesting historic monument near the start.

THE PUB

The White Horse Inn, Abbey Road, TA23 0JZ.
☎ 01984 640415   www.exmoorpubs.co.uk
A popular and attractive riverside pub with B&B. Features roaring log fires and a balcony overlooking the river.

THE WALK

1 Turn right out of the car park along **Abbey Road**. Watch out for traffic as there is no pavement. Continue to the **White Horse Inn** where you go straight on over the bridge. Pass the trout farm and after **Torre House**, turn right up a narrow lane past **Orchard House**. The route becomes steeper. Just after the brow of the hill, opposite the farm, turn right through a metal gate onto a footpath. Follow the hedgeline to the left. At the bottom go right, then down through a gate into the next field and over a stile on the left to wooden steps. Immediately swing

START: Cleeve Abbey Car Park, Washford. **Sat Nav:** TA23 0PS.

PARKING: The car park opposite Cleeve Abbey on Abbey Road.

MAP: OS Explorer OL9 Exmoor. **Grid Ref:** ST046407.

TERRAIN: Several stiles and some gradients but none very steep.

left onto a path through the trees. Turn right onto a path which crosses a pretty stream. Cross the field, taking you to the lane.

❷ Take the footpath up steps just to the right, going up steeply. Cross a stile and turn left along the edge of the crop field. Proceed uphill and follow the field boundary around to the right, going up to the corner. Go left through the gap in the hedge and then right to a track. Turn right along the track. Continue for some distance along a high ridge providing good views. Head gently downhill to a stile. The route bends right taking you to a dusty lane, past cottages to the main road.

❸ Turn left and cross the road. At the **Washford Inn** turn right onto a footpath. This turns 90 degrees left at the end of the building then back right between a fence and a hedge, bringing you eventually to a road junction by the railway bridge. Proceed straight ahead along **Huish Lane**. Pass the school and cross over the **River Washford**. When you reach the main road, turn right then almost immediately (carefully) cross over and take **Quarry Road** on the left. At the junction, with **Belle Vue Road** soon after, go straight ahead onto the footpath.

❹ Pass garages going steeply up and at the concrete track go straight ahead. At the next footpath junction, go straight on over a stile. Keep right by the hedge. Cross another stile in the corner then immediately turn right onto a permissive path, keeping to the hedge on the right. There is no well-defined path here. Continue into the next field with the hedge now on the left. Go to the corner at the bottom and through the hedge to a path junction.

❺ Turn right through a shady canopy of trees. When you emerge into the field, keep left at the fork. Cross over two more stiles onto another

Guide to Somerset Pub Walks

shaded path. Continue straight on past the large metal gates, over a stile and down past the orchard on the left to **Hillside Road**, which is a stony track leading to the road. Here turn right and retrace your steps, back past the **White Horse Inn** and on to the parking area on the left.

PLACES OF INTEREST NEARBY

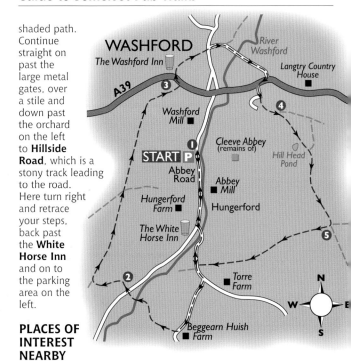

Cleeve Abbey, almost opposite the place of parking, is in the hands of English Heritage. It is a Cistercian monastery founded in the 12th century where you can learn about monastic life. The cloisters, refectory, dormitory and gatehouse have survived the ravages of Henry VIII's Dissolution virtually intact. There is a shop, toilets and picnic area outside. It is open from April to October. Also within the very close vicinity is the wildlife park, **Tropiquaria Zoo**, the **Torre Cider Farm**, the **Washford Radio Museum** and the town has a station on the **West Somerset Railway**, a heritage line with steam and diesel engines.

5 Langford Budville

4¼ miles (6.8 km)

WALK HIGHLIGHTS

A journey through countryside in the valley of the River Tone, passing the hamlet of Runnington before returning through the pretty village of Langford Budville.

THE PUB

The Martlet Inn, Langford Budville, TA21 0QZ.
☎ 01823 401330 www.themartletinn.co.uk
Freehouse and B&B with flagstone floors, cosy open fires and a pretty garden for outdoor dining.

THE WALK

1 With your back to the parking bays, head right along the road to the crossroads. Turn right onto the footpath by the signpost. Follow this track which bends right then left, and down through the trees to a stile. Turn left along the field boundary. Before the field end, turn left over another stile through trees to another stile. At the next path junction, soon after, turn sharp right down over another stile and across a meadow. Go through a gate into the next field with good views ahead. Continue on, over a stile into the next field bringing you to a gate by a lane.

Guide to Somerset Pub Walks

START: Langford Common Road. **Sat Nav:** TA21 0RW.

PARKING: There is a parking bay a little way up on Langford Common Road by an entrance to the Langford Heathfield Nature Reserve.

MAP: OS Explorer 128 Taunton & Blackdown Hills. **Grid Ref:** ST107226.

TERRAIN: A number of stiles. Paths are generally good, but can become muddy after rainfall.

2 Go left along the lane. It bends sharp left and at the next bend soon after, turn left onto the footpath, over the bridge which crosses the **River Tone**. Follow the line of the fence alongside the river to a double-gated footbridge. Go straight ahead under the telegraph poles, but before the next stile look out for a faint path going right which crosses the brook via railway sleepers. Keep left by the fence and the old beech tree, climbing uphill, and bear left into the next field. Where the clearly defined path runs out, half way along, turn right going up steeply to a gate by the lane.

3 Turn left down the lane. When you reach the road T-junction, turn left along **Bughole Lane** which goes up and downhill. At the next T-junction, turn left again, crossing the river via the road bridge. Continue uphill (watch out for approaching cars as there is no verge). At **Ramsey Farm** turn right onto a stony byway by the cottage. Proceed along this byway for over ½ mile to where it ends at the lane.

4 Turn right along the lane into the hamlet of **Runnington**. The road bends left at **Dunns Farm**. After you pass the church (which has a seat by the entrance for a rest), turn left through a gap in the hedge onto a footpath which follows the line of the telegraph poles into successive fields which you access via stiles. Langford Budville's church comes into view. At the lane turn right, then almost immediately turn left over a stile in the hedge.

5 Head across the field. The path joins a hedge to the left and at the corner, cross a footbridge with stiles each side. Continue gently up along the field boundary to the stile at the next corner and onto the road opposite **St Peter's church** (open) in the village. Turn left along the village street

18

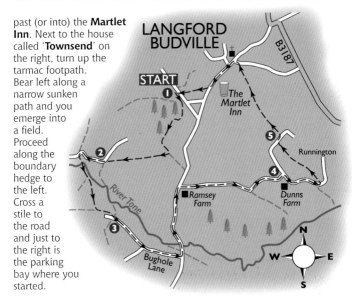

past (or into) the **Martlet Inn**. Next to the house called 'Townsend' on the right, turn up the tarmac footpath. Bear left along a narrow sunken path and you emerge into a field. Proceed along the boundary hedge to the left. Cross a stile to the road and just to the right is the parking bay where you started.

PLACES OF INTEREST NEARBY

There are two nature reserves in close proximity to the village, both owned and run by the Wildlife Trust. **Langford Heathfield** is a woodland where badgers, roe deer, a variety of birds including woodpeckers, and butterflies, along with a variety of trees, wild flowers and grasses can all be found. **Rewe Mead** is a smaller reserve on the banks of the River Tone and has the remains of the **Great Western Canal** running through it. Here there are otters, birds such as kingfishers and herons, dragonflies, frogs and toads. Unusual wetland grasses and plants are also in evidence.

At nearby **Wellington** there is a free museum run by volunteers of the **Local History and Museum Society**. It displays items concerned with the local history of the town. It regularly holds talks, events and special exhibitions.

19

River Parrett

6 Combwich
3¼ miles (5.3 km)

WALK HIGHLIGHTS
If you'd like an easy walk in a serene environment, then this route at Combwich should fit the bill. The walk starts in the quaint village, before following a wide expanse of the River Parrett, then heading off through the Steart Marshes. Here, hardly a sound can be heard apart from the occasional birdsong. There are seats along the way to stop and rest.

THE PUB
The Combwich Anchor, Riverside, TA5 2RA.
☎ 01278 653612 www.combwichanchor.co.uk
Riverside pub with good food, excellent views and a friendly atmosphere. The first and last pub stop on the River Parrett.

THE WALK
1 From the pub entrance, go left along the road and at the first bend turn right onto a bridleway which is an unmade track. The **River Parrett** soon comes into view. At the path junction, go right (to **Mendip hide**) around the football pitch. The path converges closer to the river. Pass around a metal gate. You can choose an upper or lower path, which

START: Riverside, Combwich. **Sat Nav:** TA5 2RA.

PARKING: Park by children's play area opposite the Combwich Anchor pub or further along Riverside.

MAP: OS Explorer 140 Quantock Hills & Bridgwater.
  Grid Ref: ST260424.

TERRAIN: Much of this walk is fairly flat, along wide tracks with a hard surface. No stiles.

run parallel with each other. Continue on, passing under the pylons to the wooden viewing hide where you turn left.

❷ Pass the hide, the path rejoins the bridleway, and proceed past marsh land. At the next path junction keep right passing the Mendip hide. At the next signpost keep right following the route to the **WWT car park**. At the next path junction, go left, still following the WWT car park. Cross a footbridge to the **Steart Marshes information board**, by the road opposite the car park and public toilets, then bear left and follow the path signed to **Otterhampton**, back under pylons and running parallel with the road. After a while you cross a stream and at the next signpost by the fork, you keep left, by a seat.

❸ The bridleway path runs parallel with the lane. Continue along a good, wide, hard surface which soon runs parallel with a water channel to the left. Pass another seat on the left then, further along, a hide on the right with bird identification boards and a seat. Proceed on past another seat; the winding path then turns sharp right then left. Eventually, you reach the gate at the path T-junction. Turn right. At the end of the playing field you bear left onto a grass path which bends right along by the river. At the seat, turn right up the bank to return to **Riverside** and the pub.

PLACES OF INTEREST NEARBY
Steart Marshes is a vast area of wetlands owned by the Wildfowl & Wetlands Trust (WWT). It is home to otters, butterflies, dragonflies and many varieties of migrating birds. You will pass the bird-viewing hides

along the route. These contain information and illustrations of the birds that can be seen, including black winged stilts, avocets, oystercatchers, spoonbills, egrets and many more.

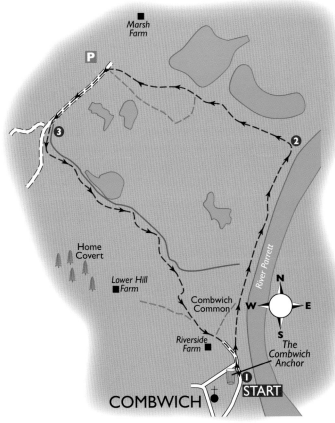

7 Kingston St Mary

5 miles (8 km)

WALK HIGHLIGHTS

If you like a challenge then this may be the walk for you. It is not only a little longer than some others in the book, but also involves some very steep climbs. Located on the edge of the Quantock Hills, the route runs from Kingston to Broomfield and back, with some wonderful distant views of the Somerset countryside.

THE PUB

The Swan, Kingston Road, TA2 8HW.
☎ 01823 451383 www.swanpubkingston.co.uk
A cosy pub in the heart of the village, known for its cask ales and traditional menu. Dog friendly.

THE WALK

1 Turn left out of the pub car park and then immediately right at the road junction (signed to **Bishops Lydeard**) using the pavement. Where the pavement runs out, continue on but watch out for traffic. After passing the turning with **Tarr Lane**, at the fork soon after, go right onto a private road (but public footpath), past **Lower Lodge**, going uphill. Near the top of the hill turn left onto a footpath going across the meadow. Continue through a metal gate onto a narrow path between fences with fine views around. Go through a metal gate to a wide track.

Guide to Somerset Pub Walks

START: The Swan, Kingston St Mary. **Sat Nav:** TA2 8HW.

PARKING: The Swan car park. Please ask the landlord's permission to park if not visiting the pub.

MAP: OS Explorer 140 Quantock Hills & Bridgwater.
   Grid Ref: ST221296.

TERRAIN: There are no stiles but a very steep, long climb up to Broomfield.

② Turn right up another private road leading to **Tetton House**. At the little path junction turn left and, before the gate entrance to the house, turn left onto a footpath, keeping left of the red beech tree. Pass through a wooden gate and continue down into the next field and go straight ahead. A valley and hill are to the left. The path widens with a fence to the right. Pass into the next field and bear left on the path gradually running alongside the fence to the left. Go through a metal gate (usually open) into the next field and keep left heading for the far corner of the field. Turn left. Pass a barn and stables leading to the road by the hotel.

③ Turn right up the little lane, part of the **Macmillan Way**. The road bends right then left. Where it bends sharp left again, turn off right onto a byway, going steeply downhill between trees to the road. Cross over and continue down the byway on the other side. Cross over a pretty ford via stepping stones and climb back uphill for some distance. The path levels out for a while and meanders through the trees and then goes uphill steeply again, an extensive climb eventually leading to the road.

④ Turn right and follow the lane around to the right, to the next road junction just past the next corner. Turn left into **Broomfield**. Pass **Fyne Court** (National Trust). Just before you reach the church turn right through a wooden gate onto a footpath going down through a field. Pass through a double metal gate and bear right. On the other side of this field look out for a metal gate where you cross a track and go back up through another gate into a horse field. Follow the fenceline to another metal gate. On passing through, cross the field and look for a stile on the other side.

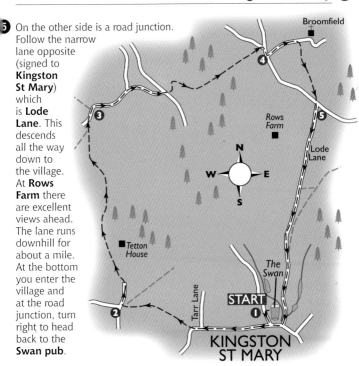

5 On the other side is a road junction. Follow the narrow lane opposite (signed to **Kingston St Mary**) which is **Lode Lane**. This descends all the way down to the village. At **Rows Farm** there are excellent views ahead. The lane runs downhill for about a mile. At the bottom you enter the village and at the road junction, turn right to head back to the **Swan pub**.

PLACES OF INTEREST NEARBY

A few miles south is the county town of **Taunton**. The medieval castle near the town centre is now the excellent **Museum of Somerset**. The museum tells the story of Somerset through the ages, but there are also special exhibitions, the **Military Museum**, a café and a shop. Free entry, but donations are welcome. Open Tuesday to Sunday.

En route at Broomfield is the National Trust property of **Fyne Court**, where you'll find gardens and a café.

8 West Monkton

3¾ miles (6 km)

WALK HIGHLIGHTS

Just a few miles from Taunton, this walk starts in the characterful village of West Monkton, before striking out into the farmland and countryside to the north of the village, and on to neighbouring Hestercombe. The return leg is on part of the East Deane Way, with a good pub near the end.

THE PUB

The Monkton Inn, Blundells Lane, TA2 8NP.
☎ 01823 412414 www.themonktoninn.co.uk
An award-winning country pub with an attractive garden and children's play area.

❶ THE WALK

Set off alongside the brick wall, passing the church entrance and keep straight ahead, up a little alleyway past some cottages. At the junction, turn right (past cottage number 2) and up into a shady canopy. At the lane, just to the left, go through a metal gate and continue gently uphill through the next gate, then between the fence and the hedge to the stile by the lane. Turn left along the lane.

START: St Augustine's Church, West Monkton. **Sat Nav:** TA2 8QT.

PARKING: Take the church access road and park in front of the parish church in the far right corner.

MAP: OS Explorer 128 Taunton & Blackdown Hills. **Grid Ref:** ST262284.

TERRAIN: One stile. Some up and downhill walking but not too steep.

❷ Where the road bends left, go straight onto a stony track. Pass a cottage then enter a wood. The path bends left. At the next cottage there are two paths. Take the one going to the left uphill to a stile and into a meadow. Go right, around the field boundary. Continue uphill. Look out for a fork, taking the unsigned left path across the middle of the field and head to the right of the mast you see in the distance. At the end, you meet a lane.

❸ Take the track opposite. Pass a pond. Just before the cottage, look out for a footpath on the right going into the woods. Follow the path through the trees to a cottage. Turn right passing between two cottages, up a track to a lane. Turn right. At the next fork turn left, along a narrow lane. At **Hill Farm** keep left through a gate. Turn left at the end (unhook and replace the electric fence handle) then immediately right by the water trough onto an unmarked footpath between two upright poles.

❹ The path runs parallel with the fence to your right. Proceed to the far corner of the field where, on the other side of the electric fence, behind the hedge, is a stile, taking you into the next field with views ahead. Keep to the hedge on the right going downhill. At the end of the field, go straight on through trees, to a T-junction with a wide track. Turn left and continue through the wood, down to a gate by **Gotton Lodge**, then more steeply down the access road to a lane junction.

❺ Take the lane almost opposite going down next to a pretty brook past **Gotton Farm**. After about 200 metres, look out for a footpath in the hedge on the left through a metal gate. Follow the field boundary through a gap in the hedge to a gate at a lane. Cross over and continue straight on into another field keeping by the hedge to the right. Halfway

Guide to Somerset Pub Walks

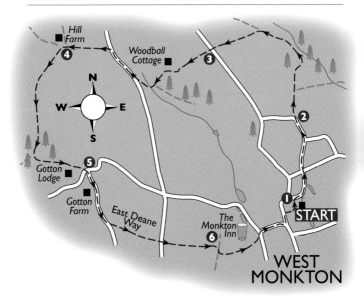

along the field, cross through the hedgeline, and continue along a crop field with the hedge now to the left.

6 At the path junction at the end of the field turn right then almost immediately left through a gate into the next meadow, then up steps through a gate leading to a path between hedge and fence. This takes you to the garden of the **Monkton Inn**. You can go around either side of the pub to the lane. Turn left and follow the road which bends around to the right (to **Coombe**). At the road junction, take the church drive opposite, bringing you back to the parking area in front of the church.

PLACES OF INTEREST NEARBY
Hestercombe House, a 16th-century mansion restored in 1875, has an orangery, an art gallery and a café.

9 North Curry

4 miles (6.4 km)

WALK HIGHLIGHTS

This is a beautiful and peaceful walk with spectacular views of the Somerset Levels. The latter section takes you to the attractive village of North Curry via a riverside path.

THE PUB

The Bird in Hand, Queen Square, TA3 6LT.

☎ 01823 490248 www.birdinhandnorthcurry.co.uk

A friendly, traditional pub and restaurant in the heart of the village. Think flagstone floors, wooden beamed ceilings and plenty of seating outside.

Guide to Somerset Pub Walks

START: St Peter & St Paul's Church, North Curry. **Sat Nav:** TA3 6LJ.

PARKING: Park in front of the church on The Fosse (road).

MAP: OS Explorer 128 Taunton & Blackdown Hills. **Grid Ref:** ST319254.

TERRAIN: Some stiles but mostly good paths.

THE WALK

1 Enter the churchyard and take the path that runs to the right of the church. Leave the graveyard via a metal gate. Bear right following the footpath arrow through a gate and along the side of the hill with distant views to the left. Keep left of a large oak and proceed to the far corner of the field, up steps and through a gate. Head uphill to another gate. Go straight ahead and over a stile to a track (**Moredon Drive**). Take the track signed to '**FARM**'.

2 Go through a wooden gate on the right and then between black fencing. Continue through a V-shaped barrier and along the field edge. Cross a stile and continue on the path through the next field. At the end, go through a gate and bear left, continuing on the path along the top of the ridge. Keep to the right of the hedge. Go through the gate into the next field, this time keep to the left of the hedge. Cross a track by a seat where you can stop to admire the views. Go through a gate on the right and at the end of the field go through a gate and down steps, then over a stile soon after. Enter the next field by the solar panels, ending at a gate by the trees.

3 Take the left fork through the trees to a track by the woodland information board. Turn left down the track (turn right if you wish to visit the **Coates English Willow Visitor Centre** en route), through gates and crossing a water channel to go up a bank to the **River Tone**. Turn left. Go through a gate by an information board and continue through more gates, along by the river for about a mile. Eventually you reach the road.

4 Turn left along the road. After about ¼ mile, turn left onto a footpath running along a dusty track between water channels. Turn right crossing the water channel via a gate (step over a low electric fence), and proceed

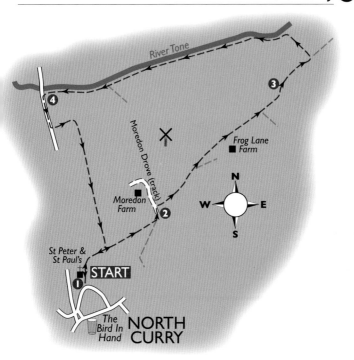

along the field to a footbridge where you bear right. The church comes into view. At the end of the field, cross a gated bridge and then head through a field of scrub to another gate where you turn right. Retrace your steps back to the church where you started.

PLACES OF INTEREST NEARBY

At the **Coates English Willow Visitor Centre** in nearby Stoke St Gregory you can visit the willow shop and museum or watch willow-weaving displays. There is also a café, shops and toilets. Free parking.

31

10 Dowlish Wake

3 miles (4.5 km)

WALK HIGHLIGHTS

This short stroll starts in the splendidly named village of Dowlish Wake, before taking you through some lovely countryside to the hamlet of Kingstone and back again. We recommend making time for a stop at Perry's Cider Mills nearby.

THE PUB

The New Inn, Dowlish Wake, TA19 0NZ.
☎ 01460 52413 www.newinn-ilminster.com
In the heart of the village, this inn has two cosy bar areas, a restaurant and secluded beer garden for the warmer months.

❶ THE WALK

Turn left out of the pub car park and, at the little road junction on the bend, turn right along a narrow street. At the T-junction, just to the left, go between houses to a footpath running across the recreation ground. Over the other side, behind the goal, go through a gate and up

START: The New Inn, Dowlish Wake. **Sat Nav:** TA19 0NZ.

PARKING: In the pub car park. Please ask the landlord's permission to park if not visiting the pub.

MAP: OS Explorer 128 Taunton & Blackdown Hills. **Grid Ref:** ST375123.

TERRAIN: A few stiles and some wet ground so appropriate footwear is needed.

alongside the hedge to the left. At the far corner go through the gate into a crop field and turn right alongside the hedge to the right. At the hedge corner, bear left, going diagonally across a large field towards an oak tree. Just past this, proceed through the gate in the hedge and follow the path across a meadow going into the woods. Cross the streams running through the trees to a stile and footbridge. Cross a field to a gate, followed by a bridge and a stile leading to a quiet lane.

2 Turn right along the lane, taking you gently down to a track running over a bridge amongst the trees. Go back up on a narrow path with a hard surface, which brings you to a road. Turn right along the road; there is little traffic but there is no pavement and some blind bends with hedges so keep on the right-hand side of the highway. Continue past houses and when you reach the next junction, ignore the right turning and at the T-junction soon after, turn right, (there is a verge on the right further along). **Kingstone church** on the left is usually open and has a bench for a rest in the churchyard. Opposite the church, you turn right onto a footpath.

3 The path runs across a large crop field. At the other side do not go through the gap but turn right alongside the hedge. Follow the field boundary to just past the corner and look out for a little path on the left which goes through the trees and down to some steps to the road. Turn left into the village. Proceed (carefully) down the road which bends right. Use the church path on the right running parallel with the road and then head along the pavement. At the road junction turn right over the old stone bridge. Pass the **Perry's Cider Mills** which are worth a visit (*see* **Places of Interest Nearby**). Continue along the path

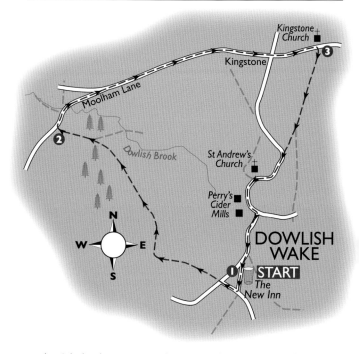

on the right by the stream. At the next road junction turn left returning to the **New Inn** and car park.

PLACES OF INTEREST NEARBY

Somerset is famous for its cider and since you're in the area, it would make sense to visit **Perry's Cider Mills**, an independently-run company that's been operating for over a hundred years. Open every day, it has a café, a museum housed in the 16th-century thatched barn and a farm shop. The shop sells a variety of bottled ciders and apple juices, which you can sample in the garden.

11 Barrington
2½ or 3¼ miles (4.2 or 5.3 km)

WALK HIGHLIGHTS
The walk begins in the heart of Barrington village with its many thatched cottages. From here, the route heads north into the countryside, then east through the National Trust property of Barrington Court. There's an option of a short walk from here or a slightly extended walk to the south. Some of the paths run through fields containing cattle. Dogs must be kept on a lead.

THE PUB
The Barrington Boar, Barrington, TA19 0JB.
☎ 01460 259281 www.thebarringtonboar.co.uk
An award-winning restaurant and bar with rooms, where you'll find a modern British menu and locally sourced produce.

THE WALK
1 With your back to the pub entrance, go right along the village road. Just past the red telephone box and converted chapel, turn right along **Bakers Lane**. This bends left and becomes a track. Follow the footpath arrow over a stile next to the gate and into a meadow. Continue over a stile into the next field and at the footpath junction, keep right over

35

Guide to Somerset Pub Walks

START: The Barrington Boar. **Sat Nav:** TA19 0JB.

PARKING: Roadside in front of the church or at the pub if visiting.

MAP: OS Explorer 128 Taunton & Blackdown Hills. **Grid Ref:** ST389181.

TERRAIN: Mostly level or with gentle slopes. Some stiles.

another stile, following the path along the edge of the field. Just before the end of the field turn left through a gate and go diagonally across the field to the other side so that the hedge is to your left. Look out for a gate about halfway along the field on the left where you cross a footbridge and proceed through undergrowth to a wooden gate leading into the next meadow. This takes you to a gate by the lane.

2 Turn right on **Lawnmoor Lane**. Pass **Barrington Farm** and shortly after, turn right onto a footpath through a kissing gate by gates. After a section of open field, follow the hedge on your right. In the far corner cross a bridge. The path runs across a meadow to a gate by a lane. Turn left.

3 Pass a footpath on the right and take the next footpath up steps on the right. Follow the line of the fence to a little gate taking you through the buildings of **Barrington Court**. Go straight ahead along the concrete path, passing the entrance to the stately house and continue onto a grass path to a footbridge over the stream. Go right across the old cricket field to the pavilion, and exit the field in the corner by the scoreboard via a gate. Cross a concrete track and go through the gate on the other side, along by a brook to a cottage on **Water Street**.

4 Turn left along the lane. At the T-junction, if you want to take a short cut, go right along the village street which will take you to the start of the walk. Otherwise, for a longer walk, turn left along **Silver Street** and at the first bend take the footpath on the right, up a dusty track. At the gate by **Stream Cottage** turn right up steps and left at the end, up more steps. Go through a gate and up through a meadow of long grass. Cross a stile and go straight on, uphill to a gate at the end of the field where there is a seat to rest and admire the distant views.

⑤ Behind the seat there is a junction of paths. Take the path over a stile and soon join a track, which runs along a hedge to your right. A little further along, the path crosses over to continue along the other side of the hedge. Continue along the edge of the field. Follow the boundary of the field around to the right, going downhill and at the bottom the path continues into the next field going gently down with a steep drop on the right. The path bends left and goes up steps. Bear right going down steeply to more steps and a kissing gate. Go through another gate where you proceed between a hedge and fence to a lane. Turn left along the lane, bringing you back into the village by the church just to your right.

PLACES OF INTEREST NEARBY
Barrington Court, a Tudor manor house run by the National Trust, has beautiful gardens, a shop and café.

12 **Cheddar**

3 miles (5 km)

WALK HIGHLIGHTS

Although a relatively short walk as the crow flies, the long upward climb makes this quite a challenge. The spectacular limestone Cheddar Gorge is the deepest gorge in England and sits within an Area of Outstanding Natural Beauty. This walk takes you alongside the gorge with amazing views of the surrounding countryside.

THE PUB

The Riverside Inn, Cliff Street, BS27 3PX.
☎ 01934 742452 www.riversidecheddar.co.uk
As the name suggests, this spacious pub serving pub classics sits on the river in the middle of Cheddar. Log fires keep things cosy in winter, and there's plenty of space in the beer garden for warmer days.

THE WALK

1 Turn right out of the car park past the **Riverside Inn**. Cross the river and immediately turn right by the **Black Dog Inn**, then keep left, going

START: Cliff Street Car Park. **Sat Nav:** BS27 3PS.

PARKING: Pay & display car park on Cliff Street, next to the Riverside Inn.

MAP: OS Explorer 141 Cheddar Gorge and Mendip Hills West.
   Grid Ref: ST461535.

TERRAIN: A very steep and extensive climb during the first half of the walk. A few stiles and some difficult rocky and uneven ground when you descend.

steeply up a narrow road (The Lippiatt), alongside the stone wall to your right. Pass **Lynch Lane** and a car park, and at the next junction turn left up an unmade track between high banks. Go through four consecutive metal gates and follow the footpath signs to an open area by **Lavender Lodge**. Bear left and follow the footpath sign through three more gates and into a meadow. Go through the kissing gate at the other end.

② Continue straight ahead following a winding path between fences. The path eventually widens. Keep straight on past **Owley Woods Glamping** and at the footpath junction, go straight on uphill. Pass through a wooden gate, and go straight on, up steeply through trees. Go through another wooden gate where you are forced left up to a stile by a fallen tree. Bear right then immediately after, at the fork, keep left through the ferns. At the top turn left along a wide grass path.

③ Cross over a stile, then head through undergrowth to a wooden gate. Turn right through a kissing gate, by an information board. This is part of the **Bubwith Acres Nature Reserve**. Keep left, still going uphill steeply on a grass path for some distance. Pass through a metal gate by the information board and continue up the grass path. After the next gate, go straight on. Head gently downhill on a grass path through ferns and heathland to a path junction. Turn left on a sandy path through the reserve.

④ Pass through a tall wooden gate then a rock section of the route with magnificent views ahead. To the right is **Cheddar Gorge**. Continue

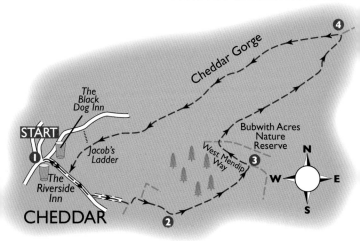

downhill for quite a distance. The path descends steeply in places so watch your footing on the stones and rocks scattered throughout the path. When you near the bottom, pass through a gate to the lookout tower. To the right are the steep steps known as **Jacob's Ladder** which lead down to the gorge. Bear left at the tower. Proceed down a narrow path to the concrete track by **Lynch Cottage**. Turn right down the track, and at the road junction turn right again. Retrace your steps back over the road bridge to Cheddar town.

PLACES OF INTEREST NEARBY

Lying on the edge of the Mendips, Cheddar is famous for its caves and its cheese. **Cheddar Man**, Britain's oldest complete skeleton dating from before 7,000 BC, was found inside **Gough's Cave**. The cave has stalactites, stalagmites and underground streams and lakes. Cheddar is also home to the **Museum of Prehistory and Dreamhunters – The Adventures of Early Man**. You can watch cheddar cheese being made at the **Cheddar Gorge Cheese Company**.

13 Wookey Hole

3½ miles (5.8 km)

WALK HIGHLIGHTS

Wookey Hole is very popular due to the attraction of the caves and the beautiful Mendip Hills that surround this area. This walk takes you steeply up the hills to the north where there are wonderful distant views across to Wells.

THE PUB

The Wookey Hole Inn, High Street, BA5 1BP.
☎ 01749 676677   www.wookeyholeinn.com
A very popular restaurant, bar and hotel serving locally sourced organic produce. Design and decor is inspired by the local caves.

THE WALK

1 With your back to the church, head right along the **High Street** past **Wookey Hole caves** entrance and car park. Where the road bends sharp left, turn right up **School Hill** (cul de sac). Go steeply up and at the top, go through a metal gate onto a wide track. Follow this up between fences, through another gate where the path veers left, and then up steeply and over a stile. Continue straight up through a thicket

41

Guide to Somerset Pub Walks

START: High Street, Wookey Hole. **Sat Nav:** BA5 1BS.

PARKING: Park on the High Street in front of St Mary Magdalene's church.

MAP: OS Explorer 141 Cheddar Gorge and Mendip Hills West.
  Grid Ref: ST532475.

TERRAIN: Mostly good paths but many ups and downs. The byway at the end of the walk is often wet and muddy so robust, waterproof footwear is necessary.

into a meadow. Cross another stile into the next field, then another stile on the other side of the field. Go straight, heading steeply upwards amongst gorse bushes. Just before the next stile turn right.

2 Follow the path that runs through the cow field parallel to the field wall. There are spectacular distant views to the right. Cross a stile at the other end and bear right, heading diagonally across the field to a stile by a metal gate, leading to a sheltered path through the trees going down quite steeply. Pass through a metal gate onto a wide track. At the next gate the path forks. Take the left option across the middle of the meadow, down through another gate. Bear left keeping the electric fence to your right and swing right at the hedge and follow the field boundary down to a stile by a little lane.

3 Turn left along the lane. Soon after turn right onto a private road, carefully cross by the cattle grid and follow the track for a while. Just before where the path bends right by the telegraph pole, go left across the field heading for the telegraph pole in the middle of the field. At the pole, go straight on looking for a gate in the hedge on the other side of the field. Climb steeply to a kissing gate, taking you between buildings of **Manor Farm** and another gate to a road (**Old Bristol Road**). Turn right along the road and uphill to where it bends left. Here turn right through a kissing gate onto a footpath.

4 The path runs along the boundary of a meadow, then over a stile and down through trees between steep banks. The path becomes a

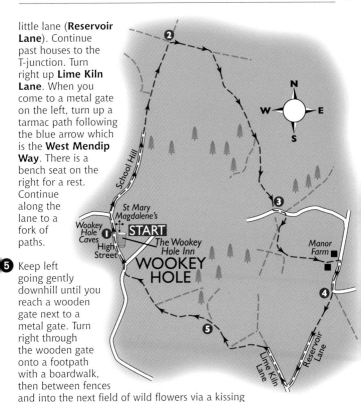

little lane (**Reservoir Lane**). Continue past houses to the T-junction. Turn right up **Lime Kiln Lane**. When you come to a metal gate on the left, turn up a tarmac path following the blue arrow which is the **West Mendip Way**. There is a bench seat on the right for a rest. Continue along the lane to a fork of paths.

5 Keep left going gently downhill until you reach a wooden gate next to a metal gate. Turn right through the wooden gate onto a footpath with a boardwalk, then between fences and into the next field of wild flowers via a kissing gate. This takes you to a road. Turn right into the village and back to the **High Street** where you started.

PLACES OF INTEREST NEARBY

Wookey Hole caves, located at the start of the walk, are limestone caverns with the River Axe running through them.

43

14 Glastonbury

4½ miles (7.1 km)

WALK HIGHLIGHTS

This town might be famous for its music festival, but as you'll see it's also a cracking place for a country stroll. Starting in the heart of town, this route heads out into countryside using lanes and footpaths, before climbing to the Tor to take in magnificent views of Somerset.

THE PUB

The Riflemans Arms, Chilkwell Street, BA6 8DB.
☎ 01458 831023 www.facebook.com/TheRifes
A 16th-century traditional pub with cosy fires inside, and outside seating for the warmer weather.

THE WALK

1 From the car park go right to the top of **Butt Close** and turn right (along **Wells Road**). Cross over at the crossing and take the next turning left up **Bove Town**. Continue uphill to the junction and follow the road around left into **Old Wells Road**. Proceed along the pavement, continuing uphill before descending. Where the pavement runs out, watch out for fast moving traffic. Just before **32 Hillside Cottage**, look out for a very narrow concealed footpath on the right, taking you into a meadow.

START: Butt Close Car Park. **Sat Nav:** BA6 9HY.

PARKING: The pay & display car park is just off the main high street.

MAP: OS Explorer 141 Cheddar Gorge and Mendip Hills West.
   Grid Ref: ST501390.

TERRAIN: A long steep climb up to the Tor and a few stiles.

❷ Go left in the field through a metal gate and bear left again through the meadow to a stile by an electric fence and into the next meadow. On the other side of the field, a stile brings you to a lane. Turn right along the lane past **Lower Brindham Farm**. The lane bends sharply both left and right. Pass **Brindham Farm** and **The Orchard**. At the next sharp left-hand bend, turn off right onto a private road (but public footpath) signed to **Paddington Farm Trust**, along a stony track.

❸ **Glastonbury Tor** soon comes into view. The track bends right and comes to a junction where you turn left onto the signed footpath. Cross a stile into the next field, then cross a stream via three consecutive stiles. In the next meadow head for the enclosed tree in the middle of the field and, just past this, go through a kissing gate. Continue between a hedge and fence to the next gate, following a stony track, signed to **The Tor**. Pass an information board on the right. Keep straight on to reach a kissing gate next to large metal gates.

❹ Turn right up a tarmac track, going steeply uphill for some distance. Near the top is a seat for a rest with lovely distant views. Continue on until you reach the road junction. Turn right past a seat and information board, and soon after turn left onto a footpath which takes you up a steep path and steps all the way to the top of the Tor. Here you can enjoy magnificent views all around. From the church tower on the top, take the concrete path which goes down in the opposite direction from the one you came up.

❺ At the road at the bottom, turn right past the **White Spring**. Go steeply uphill and take the next turning on the left by Bridge View house, up a narrow lane. Where the lane bends right, turn left to a gate and stone

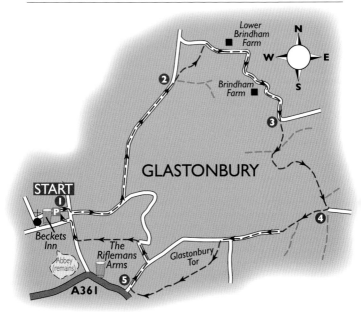

path. You will reach the street via a kissing gate at the bottom. Go left to the main road opposite **Abbey House**. For the **Riflemans Arms** turn left and then left again at the mini roundabout. If not visiting the pub, turn right and go straight on, turning left into the **High Street**. To return to the car park, look for an alley a little way down on the right next to **Peking Place**. This will take you directly to the car park.

PLACES OF INTEREST NEARBY
Somerset Rural Life Museum and **Glastonbury Lake Village Museum** are both worth a visit. The town has some unique and quirky shops and there are often street artists to watch at **Market Cross** at the west end of the High Street.

15 Kingsdon

5½ miles (9 km)

WALK HIGHLIGHTS
A pleasant country walk from the sleepy village of Kingsdon to the Charlton villages and back past the grand Lytes Cary Manor.

THE PUB
Kingsdon Inn, Chapel Hill, TA11 7LG.
☎ 01935 840543 www.kingsdoninn.co.uk
An attractive thatched pub with a pretty garden, renowned for its good food.

THE WALK
1 With your back to the pub entrance, turn right and follow the road to the left, alongside the recreation ground (**Manor Road**). At the next junction turn right up **Silver Street**. Go to the end and turn right. Pass **All Saints' church** and some pretty cottages. At the next junction pass **North Street** and immediately after, where the road bends left, go straight on, up a lane with hedges on both sides. Proceed gently uphill.

47

Guide to Somerset Pub Walks

START: Kingsdon Inn. **Sat Nav:** TA11 7LG.

PARKING: Kingsdon Inn car park, with the landlord's permission.

MAP: OS Explorer 129 Yeovil & Sherborne. **Grid Ref:** ST518261.

TERRAIN: Two stiles, some uneven ground, mostly gentle gradients.

When you reach a crossroad of tracks, go straight ahead following the blue bridleway arrow.

2 Continue along the track. The path goes gently down with good distant views to the right. At the next junction the right of way continues to the left, going into the woods. At the next fork keep right. Proceed along the path through the trees. The rutted path descends more steeply, then bends sharp left. It continues down to a junction of public paths. Turn right through a gap by a gate, onto the **Macmillan Way**.

3 The line of the path goes diagonally across a field to the right, but if the field is ploughed, go right and follow the field boundary as it takes you left along a wide grass path. At the far end you cross a bridge over a stream and continue across a meadow to a stile. Turn right along the road for a short distance and then left through a gate soon after onto a footpath signed to **Charlton Court**. Pass through a kissing gate and go along by the fence, through another gate then soon on to a gravel path leading to a lane.

4 Turn left along the lane, but soon after turn right onto a footpath next to the stable, signed to the war memorial. The path runs between fields to a busy road. Turn right along the road but a short way down look out for a gap in the hedge on the left. Follow this to a stile going into the next field by the church. Cross a stile at the other end to the lane and go right to a T-junction where you turn left along a lane.

5 At the next bend, turn down **Chessels Lane**. Go to the end and turn right at the T-junction. Take the next turning left, which is a bridleway signed to the **Fosse Way**. This is **Ridgeway Lane** which you follow for over ½ mile. About 200 metres after the barrier turn right through a gap in the hedge onto a path running across a field. It later continues along the field edge.

6 Go gently downhill to where the path bends left then, before you reach the **Lytes Carey** access road, keep right alongside the crop. At the end, pass through the hedge to a road. Turn left then, just past the entrance to Lytes Carey, turn right into a lane leading to **Kingsdon** village. Proceed along the lane passing over a stream and continue for another ½ mile. As you enter the village go left at the fork. Continue past **Mow Barton road** and follow the road around to the right to return to the **Kingsdon Inn**.

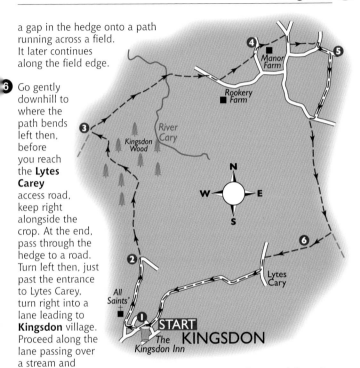

PLACES OF INTEREST NEARBY

Lytes Cary, now in the hands of the National Trust, is a medieval manor house first built in the 14th century but extended over the centuries and restored in 1907. The house and chapel are open to the public and there are beautifully kept gardens and a café.

16 Montacute

2½ miles (4.2 km)

WALK HIGHLIGHTS

Much of this walk is within the boundaries of Ham Hill Country Park, so the route is often on parkland paths rather than public footpaths. There are wonderful views from the top of the park and the popular village has quaint hamstone-built cottages and houses.

THE PUB

The Phelips Arms, The Borough, TA15 6XB.
☎ 01935 822557   www.phelipsarms.co.uk
Characterful village pub set in a pretty 17th-century hamstone building. Expect home-cooked traditional pub fare.

THE WALK

1 Go left from the car park along **Middle Street** past honey-coloured hamstone cottages and the village hall. At the parish church turn left onto a private road (but public footpath). At **Abbey Farm** soon after, turn right (signed to **Hedgecock Hill Wood**) and go through a wooden gate and keep left but follow around the base of **St Michael's Hill**. In the far corner of the field, ignore the kissing gate but cross over a

50

START: South Street, Montacute. **Sat Nav:** TA15 6XB.

PARKING: Park on South Street opposite the Phelips Arms (free for two hours).

MAP: OS Explorer 129 Yeovil & Sherborne. **Grid Ref:** ST498169.

TERRAIN: Only one stile, and one steep climb but some uneven ground towards the end of the walk.

stile to the right, into a wood and under the fallen tree, going uphill steeply. Continue uphill and keep left at the fork. Pass through a gate and proceed straight ahead across a meadow.

❷ Go through two more gates and straight on again with a fence to the right. Swing left across the large field of the country park on a path which terminates at the lane and a parking area by **Ham Hill Country Park**. Cross over and, a little to the right, by the Ham Hill stone sign, take the path to the left through a gate. Keep left on a grass path that follows the line of the fence which runs parallel to a road. Continue for

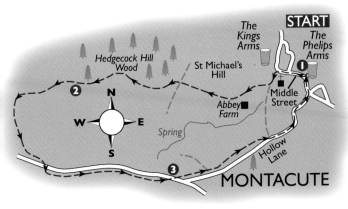

Guide to Somerset Pub Walks

some distance. At the next gate go steeply down and follow the path along the fence. At the end of the field, go through a gate on the left to a lane.

3 Cross the road and go through the kissing gate next to the metal gate onto a footpath. There are good views of **St Michael's Hill** and **Montacute** village. Pass a seat then continue through a gate, going straight ahead. Watch your footing as the path is rather uneven here. Pass into the next field and descend to where you exit on the right to a lane. Go down the lane which bends left then right to a road junction. Turn left which takes you back past the **TV Radio Toy Museum** to the car park.

PLACES OF INTEREST NEARBY
Montacute House, run by the National Trust, was built in local hamstone by Tudor Master of the Rolls and House of Commons Speaker, Sir Edward Phelips. It has the longest long gallery in England. There are gardens, parkland, a shop, a café and toilets.

Cadbury Castle

17 South Cadbury

3½ miles (5.8 km)

WALK HIGHLIGHTS
A peaceful walk from the village of South Cadbury to neighbouring Sutton Montis. The route explores the mysterious Bronze and Iron Age hillfort of Cadbury Castle, said to be the stronghold of King Arthur.

THE PUB
The Camelot, Chapel Rd, BA22 7EX.
☎ 01963 441685   www.camelotpub.co.uk
A family-friendly pub with modern decor serving traditional pub favourites made from locally sourced ingredients.

THE WALK
1 Turn left out of the car park and proceed along the lane. Pass a road on the left and look out for a footpath a little further down on the left. Cross a stile, then another, crossing the bridge over a babbling brook. When

Guide to Somerset Pub Walks

START: Cadbury Castle Car Park, Church Road. **Sat Nav:** BA22 7HA.

PARKING: If Cadbury Castle Car Park is full you can park opposite the church or at the Camelot if you are using the pub.

MAP: OS Explorer 129 Yeovil & Sherborne. **Grid Ref:** ST631253.

TERRAIN: A few stiles, but relatively good paths and easy walking.

you reach the corrugated shelter, go right through a metal gate and then turn left to follow the footpath running alongside the wire fence to your left. At the next metal gate there is a sign for two footpaths. Continue on the one running straight on with a bank to your left.

2 Continue to a double set of metal gates, where you turn right. Head downhill on a wide track between fences. This grass path converts to a dusty track which passes between farm buildings, with a mill wheel to the right. Head up a narrow lane to a road junction. Turn right, going down the lane which bends left. At the next road junction, turn right (signed to **South Cadbury**).

3 A little further down on the left, on the corner with a farm track, there is a double stile on a footpath. Follow this going diagonally across the meadow to a metal gate in the far corner (you will need to undo the chain to get through the gate). Continue diagonally across the next horse field to a stile in the far corner which soon leads through trees to a lane. Turn left along the lane passing the **Old Rectory** and at the T-junction, turn right.

4 Pass cottages and the quaint **Holy Trinity Church** in **Sutton Montis**. Continue along the lane which is part of the **Leland Trail**. Cross over a brook and pass mighty oak trees to where the road bends sharp left. Here you turn right onto a footpath which follows the field boundary on a wide grass path. **Cadbury Castle** is the hill to your right. Continue along the footpath which converts to a wide track, then later to a lane, taking you to the crossroads and the **Camelot pub**. Turn right going gently uphill to take you back past the entrance to **Cadbury Castle** and the car park on the left.

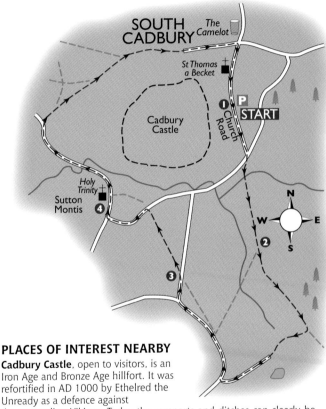

PLACES OF INTEREST NEARBY

Cadbury Castle, open to visitors, is an
Iron Age and Bronze Age hillfort. It was
refortified in AD 1000 by Ethelred the
Unready as a defence against
the marauding Vikings. Today the ramparts and ditches can clearly be
seen and archaeological artefacts from the site are in the **Museum of
Somerset** in Taunton.

The next village to the west is **Sparkford**, which is home to the
International Motor Museum.

18 Castle Cary
4 miles (6.4 km)

WALK HIGHLIGHTS
This route in and around Castle Cary ticks off everything required of a decent Somerset walk: hills, views and time to explore a quaint market town.

THE PUB
The George Hotel, Market Place, BA7 7AH.
☎ 01963 350761   www.thegeorgehotelcastlecary.co.uk
A 15th-century inn with modern decor inside, offering both a restaurant and a bar menu.

THE WALK
❶ Take the road opposite the church (**The Park**) in front of the junior school going uphill. Just the other side of the school building, turn left onto a footpath to **Cary Hill**. Go through a metal gate and between fences to a wooden gate. Cross a track via gates either side, then head steeply uphill. Just before the next gate, bear right onto a path running uphill with a barbed wire fence to the left. Follow the field boundary, going left then, at the footpath junction by the metal gate swing right.

START: All Saints' Church, Church Street. **Sat Nav:** BA7 7ED.

PARKING: Roadside on Church Street in front of the church.

MAP: OS Explorer 142 Shepton Mallet and Mendip Hills East.
   Grid Ref: ST639320.

TERRAIN: No stiles but a steep climb at the beginning of the walk.

Continue uphill on a grass track. There are seats to the right. Proceed along the ridge to the telescope station.

2 Start to descend between fences. At the bottom, cross a track, and then go straight on to a gate by a lane (**Park Avenue**). Keep ahead to a junction and turn right onto the main road (cross over to use the pavement). Soon after, turn left into **Cockhill Elm Lane**. Go to the end and continue on a grass path, over a stile and into a large meadow. Head down across the field. About a third of the way along from the right corner there is a gate in the hedgeline which you go through. Turn right to join a shady byway. This runs for some distance and ends at a tarmac track. Turn left.

3 The track bends left and takes you to a lane. Turn right along the lane and keep ahead until you reach a crossroads. Turn left into **Blackworthy Road** and, just after the entrance to the industrial estate, take the footpath on the right (to **Clanville**) going over a little footbridge. This is a wide path that swings right and runs parallel with the railway line. At the next path junction go right, following the line of the metal green fence. At the metal gates turn left onto a footpath going over a footbridge.

4 At the fork, keep right across the middle of the meadow. On the other side go through the gap in the hedge and continue across the middle of the field, through the next gap in the hedge where you go left across the field going gently uphill, through another gap, bringing you up to a main road. Cross over and turn left along the pavement. Take the next turning on the right, **Almsford Close**. Follow this around to the wooden fence where you turn left (by no. 31). Swing right along the side of the field up to a metal gate at the end of the lane.

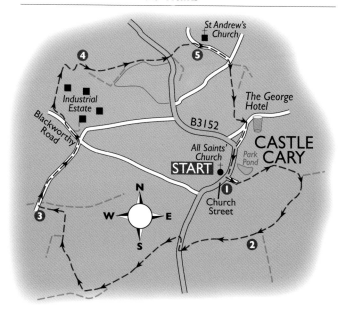

⑤ Turn right onto a tarmac footpath taking you to the steps up to a path junction by **St Andrew's church**. Turn right passing a play area. Continue between houses and a fence into **Priory View** and keep ahead to a road. Take the footpath opposite into the recreation ground. At the end proceed down the lane by the stone wall and past houses into the town by the round tower. Bear left to the **High Street** where you turn right, passing the **George Hotel** which is opposite **Market House**. To return to the car keep ahead along the main street past the petrol station and back into **Church Street**.

PLACES OF INTEREST NEARBY

The **Castle Cary Museum** is housed in **Market House**, a grand Victorian building which you pass at the end of your walk.

19 Cranmore

4 miles (6.4 km)

WALK HIGHLIGHTS
A walk from the little village of Cranmore, on the edge of the Mendip Hills, using part of the East Mendip Way. You may hear the toot of a steam engine along the way.

THE PUB
Strode Arms, East Cranmore Lane, BA4 4QJ.
☎ 01749 880303   www.thestrodearms.co.uk
Attractive village pub with a terrace to the front overlooking the pond and small garden to the rear.

THE WALK
1 With your back to the car park turn left along the highway (**Piers Road**) and continue ahead at the road junction, passing **Church Lane** and heading uphill. At the main road, carefully cross over to the road opposite and then immediately turn left over a stile into the recreation ground. Head to the left of the field by the tennis court and follow the field boundary around to the right, to a gate in the hedge on the left.

Guide to Somerset Pub Walks

START: East Somerset Railway – Cranmore Station. **Sat Nav:** BA4 4QP.

PARKING: Cranmore Station car park is open during weekends, Bank Holidays, Wednesdays and Thursdays from March to October. Otherwise, park in the area outside the gates or at the pub around the corner.

MAP: OS Explorer 142 Shepton Mallet and Mendip Hills East.
  Grid Ref: ST667430.

TERRAIN: There are several stiles, some with steps. Otherwise, some uphill and downhill climbs but not too steep.

Once through the gate keep right following the line of the hedge, then pass through another gate in the hedge. Go straight across the field to a kissing gate and in the next field keep right along the hedge. Where this ends, keep straight on to the corner and a gap in the wall. Keep to the right hedge, going over a stile into a meadow. Continue over a stile into another field then another stile on the other side into a field of grass. This takes you to a cottage by a lane.

2 Turn right along **Farrington Lane** to the T-junction. Take the footpath opposite over the cattle grid. A concrete path leads to a cottage, where you keep right onto a grass path. Go between a barrier into a field to pass another house and keep ahead along their access drive. Pass another house and then turn right at the black gates onto a footpath which goes up through a meadow to a gate. Proceed straight across the next field to a barrier (which you lift) and a stone stile into a small field with caravans. Pass through a wooden gate into a grass field. On the other side there is a stone stile bringing you to a road.

3 Head down **Ball Lane** just to the left. At the road junction at the end, take the footpath opposite, over a stile by a metal gate. Bear right just before the metal gate, going into a field and up a hillock, then through a kissing gate. Go across the grass meadow to a gap. In the next field, head for the right corner to a gate, then follow the path going diagonally right across the field. At the far corner go gently uphill across the middle of a meadow to a gate half way along the hedgeline. Enter a wooded area where you reach a path junction. Turn right down through the trees.

4 Continue downhill to a stile where you go left out into the open. Follow the path into the next field, then between gates and along the edge of a field with a hedge on the right. Cross a track by **Dean Farm** and go straight on, over a bridge. A yellow arrow guides you into the next field. Continue on the path across the

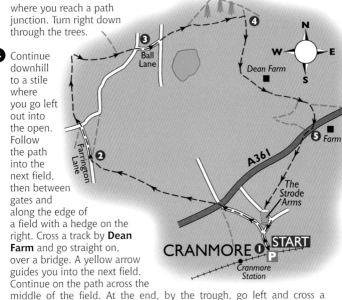

middle of the field. At the end, by the trough, go left and cross a stile to a drive. Turn right over the cattle grid and past houses to a main road.

5 Turn right, past **Pawelski Close** and the old chapel. Immediately after, carefully cross over the main road and take the footpath on the left going to the right of a large oak tree. Head for the church and, in the far corner of the field, go through a gate and across a crop field taking you to a cul-de-sac with houses. Turn left at the end then down to the next T-junction where you turn right. After **Strode Arms pub** turn left at the next junction to return to the car park.

PLACES OF INTEREST NEARBY

For train enthusiasts, a visit to **Cranmore railway station** is a must.

20 **Nunney**

3 miles (5 km)

WALK HIGHLIGHTS

Nunney is a delightful village, dominated by the medieval castle. This walk includes part of the Macmillan Way, which runs alongside the Nunney Brook up to the neighbouring village of Lower Whatley and back through open countryside ending in the village centre.

THE PUB

The George Inn, Church Street, BA11 4LW.
☎ 01373 836458   www.thegeorgeinnnunney.com
Grade II-listed inn with a riverside terrace. Features roaring fireplaces, a walled garden and a location right opposite England's smallest medieval castle.

THE WALK

1 From the car park turn left (**Castle Hill**) towards the village. After 100 metres turn left through a gate onto a tree-lined footpath. Go up through another gate and proceed between fences to a third gate which brings you into a meadow. Bear right following the path across the middle of the field. At the path crossroads, by the wooden tortoise,

START: Nunney Castle car park. **Sat Nav:** BA11 4NL.

PARKING: The car park on Castle Hill.

MAP: OS Explorer 142 Shepton Mallet and Mendip Hills East.
  Grid Ref: ST735457.

TERRAIN: No stiles or steep gradients. Parts may be muddy underfoot
  after heavy rain, particularly the path by the river.

turn right and cross the river (**Nunney Brook**) via the gate on the left.
The path swings left by another tortoise.

2 Follow the line of the river on the left. Continue for some distance to
a path junction. Turn left along a wide track, crossing the river. Almost
immediately turn right onto another shady path through the trees
which now follows the other side of the river. Eventually the path goes
uphill to a path junction. Turn right over the river. The path swings right
again and just before the metal gate turn left through a wooden swing
gate. Bear right following around the boundary of a crop field.

3 Continue into the next field but this time keep to the left. Go uphill but
soon after go through a gate on the left; the footpath goes diagonally
across the field to the right corner (it may be easier to go right around
the field edge). In the far corner, a junction of four fields, go right onto
a grass path with the hedge to the left. Go gently down to the gap
ahead. Here you bear right onto a path running diagonally across the
field to the other side where you pass through a double set of gates in
the hedge and then go left around the field edge.

4 Continue to the end of a long field (crossing a track near the end), to
another wooden swing gate and keep right along the hedge. Go to the
end of the field through a gate and cross a farm track into the next
field. Halfway along, the path diverts through a gate on the right into
the trees. Continue to a metal swing gate where the path bends sharp
left, then right soon after through another gate. Proceed down onto a
concrete path past houses. At the road turn left. At the T-junction turn
right into the village. Pass the war memorial, pond, **All Saints' Church**

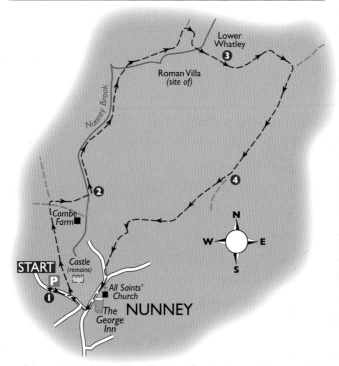

and the castle. At the road junction just after the **George Inn** turn right, back up to the car park on the right.

PLACES OF INTEREST NEARBY

Nunney Castle was built in the 14th century by Sir John Delamare, from spoils gained during the Hundred Years' War. On each corner there are four large round towers and a moat. It was heavily damaged by Cromwell's men during the English Civil War and later fell into ruin. It is now maintained by English Heritage and is free to visit.